Peak Present
Engage Your Audic

By Robert Hellmann, P

Published by:
Robert Hellmann LLC, New York, USA

THANK YOU FOR YOUR PURCHASE

Trademarks
Peak Presentations™ is a federally registered trademark of
Robert Hellmann LLC
RESULTS™ is a federally registered trademark of Robert Hellmann LLC.
The Five O'Clock Club® is a federally registered trademark of
The Five O'Clock Club, Inc.
PowerPoint® is a federally registered trademark of
the Microsoft Corporation, Inc.
YouTube® is a federally registered trademark of Google, Inc.
All terms mentioned in this book that are known to be trademarks or
service marks have been appropriately capitalized. Use of a term in
this book should not be regarded as affecting the validity of any
Trademark or Service Mark.

Photos and Illustrations
All photos and illustrations on the cover and on pages 36 and 84 are
licensed through iStock (www.istockphoto.com). The photos and

---

illustrations on pages 21, 27, 33, 34, 38, 43, 58 and 89 are licensed through shutterstock (www.shutterstock.com)

Limit of Liability/Disclaimer of Warranty:
This Book is sold with the following understanding:
While the publisher and author have used their best efforts in preparing this Book, they make no representations or warranties with respect to the accuracy or completeness of the contents of this Book and specifically disclaim any implied warranties of merchantability or fitness for a particular purpose. No warranty may be created or extended by sales representatives or written sales materials. The advice and strategies contained herein may not be suitable for your situation. Neither the publisher nor author shall be liable for any damages arising herefrom. The fact that an organization or website is referred to in this work as a citation and/or a potential source of further information does not mean that the author endorses the information the organization or website may provide or recommendations it may make. Further, readers should be aware that internet websites listed in this work may have changed or disappeared between when this work was written and when it is read.

TABLE OF CONTENTS

About the Author

As President of **Hellmann Career Consulting**, Robert Hellmann provides career services to individuals and organizations. He's a certified Five O'Clock Club Senior Career Coach and Executive Coach as well as an adjunct Instructor at New York University. Rob has delivered "Presentation & Pitch," "Social Media," "Creativity" and "Employee Engagement" seminars to global Fortune 500 companies. He also runs weekly career strategy groups for c-level executives on behalf of the Club. In his private coaching practice, Rob has helped thousands of individuals to achieve career and presentation success.

Rob's background includes over 20 years of experience in Career Development, Organizational Development and Marketing. His clients and employers include American Express, JP Morgan Chase, the Federal Reserve Bank of New York and the Audubon Society. He has developed career-training programs for higher-education including Columbia University, Harvard Business School, New York University, Fordham University, Montclair State University, Baruch College and Pace University.

Rob's career-related insights and commentary have appeared in *The New York Times, Forbes, The Washington*

Post, Money Magazine, the Chicago Tribune, CNBC.com, NBC News, ABC News and more.

Active in non-profit organizations, Rob is on the board of the Association of Talent Development's (ATD) New York chapter, and has chaired Program Committees for the NY Chapter of the Marketing Executives Networking Group (MENG). He has also worked with the Big Brother/Big Sister program to offer career-related support.

Rob combines his marketing background with his training and coaching experience to help individuals present themselves effectively, and organizations improve employee communication. Feel free to contact him at rob@hellmannconsulting.com, or visit his website at www.hellmannconsulting.com.

"According to most studies, people's number one fear is public speaking. Number two is death. Death is number two. Does that sound right? This means to the average person, if you go to a funeral, you're better off in the casket than doing the eulogy."
Jerry Seinfeld

"Make thyself a craftsman in speech, for thereby thou shalt gain the upper hand."
Inscription found in a 3,000 year-old Egyptian Tomb

Introduction

Hello and welcome. The journey you are about to take is split into four parts. In the first part (Chapter 1), we'll cover what does and doesn't make for a "peak" presentation. In Chapters 2 through 9, we'll look at how to apply the *RESULTS* methodology. In Chapter 10, we'll move on to how to adapt the *RESULTS* methodology to your pitch, which is essentially a mini presentation. Finally, in Chapters 11, 12 and 13, we'll cover some additional tips on dealing with anxiety, organizing your presentation and optimizing the physical, "mechanical" aspects of your presentation.

Before I reveal the secrets to a great presentation, let me share with you a little of my background (beyond what's in the "About the Author" section) and what inspired me to write this book.

I have delivered countless presentations in my career. These presentations have consistently received top survey scores, great email and verbal feedback, referrals and requests for repeat engagements. In fact, my career hinges on my being able to deliver a powerful presentation, so I have continued to hone my skill through observation, research and practice.

The impetus for writing this book, however, came from my frustration with the quality of presentation skills training out there. Too much of the training I've observed and experienced focuses on the mechanics as the key to a great presentation. By "mechanics," I mean things like where you stand on the stage, lighting, posture, vocal quality, etc. These aspects of presenting routinely comprise the bulk of training. While important, the mechanics will only get you so far; the keys to presentation greatness lie elsewhere (as you will see in Chapter 1).

This book addresses this gap in training; it will show you how you can go beyond the mechanics to truly make your presentations powerful, memorable, and effective. The book's contents primarily represent both a summary of my field-tested experience and my study of great (and not-so great) presenters.

Now on with the show!

Chapter 1: Defining "Peak Presentations"

"You can speak well if your tongue can deliver the message of your heart."
John Ford

When I give a presentation skills training workshop, I start off with the following slide and ask the room, "What is the number one key to a great presentation?"

Key to a Great Presentation?

1. Where you stand in the room

2. How you use your hands

3. Making eye contact with an audience

4. Using "pauses" in the right places

5. All of the above

6. None of the above

Some people select "Where you stand in the room." Others choose "How you use your hands" or "Making eye contact" or "Using pauses." Some are convinced that the answer is "All of the above." Never has someone chosen "*None of the above*," which is, in fact, the correct answer. Does this surprise you? Let me explain.

The items I have listed here are "the mechanics" of a presentation. While the mechanics can help or hurt, they are not the defining factor.

Think about it. When you leave a presentation that you thought was terrific, you're unlikely to say, "I loved where he stood on the stage," or, "I thought her arm movements really emphasized her points well," or, "his eye contact was excellent," or, "the pauses were all in the right places."

What you might say is: "That story she told was so moving," or, "Wow, that information surprised me! I never thought about it like that," or, "I feel inspired and motivated by his vision."

View the mechanics as having the potential to hurt your presentation if you get them very wrong (we will cover the most common mechanical issues in Chapter 13), but not as holding the key to a "peak presentation." For most of this book, we'll be going far beyond the mechanics.

Remember, some people are considered great presenters despite insurmountable mechanical issues. One of the best professors I ever had was blind, so he wasn't able to make eye contact. Another fantastic presenter I saw was in a wheelchair and unable to use his hands, yet he inspired everyone in his audience.

What did these and other peak presenters know that helped them to go beyond the mechanics and achieve greatness in their presentations? The next chapter provides the answer.

Chapter 2: *RESULTS* Matter

"If you don't know what you want to achieve in your presentation, your audience never will."
Harvey Diamond
(#1 Best-selling co-author, Fit for Life)

Great presenters intuitively know how to apply the *RESULTS* method in their presentations. While it's a corny acronym, it is an effective way to remember the principles that I'm going to share.

Really Simple

Engaging

Stories

Useful

Licensed

Tailored

Surprising

10

It all starts with keeping your presentation really SIMPLE. Then you need to actively ENGAGE your audience, tell STORIES (i.e. give memorable examples), make it USEFUL, be perceived as having LICENSE (i.e. expertise) and TAILOR your talk to the audience and situation. Finally, you need to employ the element of SURPRISE. Getting these seven elements into your presentation will make all the difference in how you come across.

Before we dive into each element of the *RESULTS* method, you need to clearly understand the purpose of your presentation. Ask yourself, "Why am I delivering this?" "What is my objective, and my desired outcome?"

In a business setting, there are generally two types of presentations, *influencing* and *enabling*.

Influencing may include persuading someone regarding a decision they are making, trying to sell something, or advocating for a course of action.

If you are *enabling* your audience, then your goal is to teach them a new skill, concept or way of thinking. You can consider this book an *enabling* presentation, since my primary purpose is to teach you how to become a great speaker.

While it's important to know which type of presentation

you want to give, every great talk ultimately includes elements of both. For example, in the case of this book, in order to enable you to become a peak presenter, I have to influence you to accept my ideas.

Your first step in creating a top-notch presentation is to be clear about your purpose. If you aren't clear, then the audience won't be either and then you'll have a problem.

Really Simple
Engaging
Stories
Useful
Licensed
Tailored
Surprising

What's the purpose...

Influence
or
enable?

Copyright 2013 Robert Hellmann - www.hellmannconsulting.com

Don't make the mistake one of my clients made. She came to me after she delivered a less than stellar presentation to a senior executive. She wasn't sure if she should have presented an overview of the department and how it works - in other words, an *enabling* presentation - or delivered recommendations on how to make the department more efficient - in other words, an *influencing* presentation.

She needed to do the homework ahead of time to understand what kind of information her boss was looking for. The bottom line: you need to decide in advance what you want your audience to say, feel or think following your presentation.

Once you've decided whether your presentation is primarily an enabling one or an influencing one, you're ready to move forward by bringing in each of the elements of the *RESULTS* method.

Chapter 3: Really Simple

*"Make everything as simple as possible but not
simpler...If you can't explain it simply,
you don't understand it well enough."*
Albert Einstein

Keeping things as simple as possible helps to ensure that
your message will be heard and understood. Let's look at
some examples to illustrate what I mean by "simple," using
charts and tables that might be included in presentation
slides.

Gross Revenue is Still Depressed

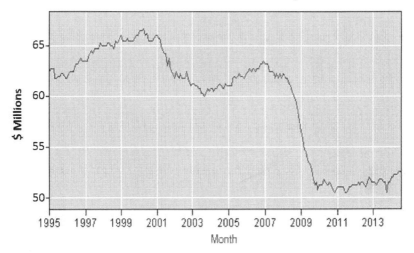

How quickly do you understand the point this chart is trying to make? For me, it takes about three seconds. It's clearly titled so that you understand: "Gross Revenue is Still Depressed." And you see just one line that drops off steeply beginning in 2008, and then stays low. Pretty clear.

Now take a look at this next slide.

Table 1. Estimates of Purchases Multiple for Spending*

Period	Multiplier	Usage Factor
1930-2014	0.65	-0.11
	(0.09)	(0.09)
1950-2014	0.41	-0.19
	(0.22)	(0.20)
1960-2014	0.23	-0.05
	(0.75)	(0.19)
1940-1950	0.59	-0.07
	(0.17)	(0.04)
1950-1956	0.58	-0.12
	(0.46)	(0.01)
1940-1945	0.46	-0.13
	(0.20)	(0.08)
1946-1950	0.49	-0.08
	(0.18)	(0.09)

* Numbers in parentheses are standard errors

How quickly do you get this one? There are *a lot* of numbers in this table. It's the opposite of simple. You don't want to show a table like this while you are speaking because it's going to compete with what you are saying. **You don't want your slides to compete with your speech for your audience's attention.** While you may need to share detailed handouts, your visual projections should not have the same level of detail or the audience will be pulled away from your presentation as they try to decipher each slide.

If you absolutely must show all the detail on a complex slide, consider a) animating it so that you highlight a new part of the slide after you have finished talking about the previous part, or b) splitting the information into multiple slides.

For example, in one presentation skills training class I was leading, I analyzed a participant's slide for an important product review presentation. On the slide he listed six products, with a picture of each and an accompanying description. Way too much information for one slide! For him the solution was easy, however: he simply split up that one slide into six, one for each product.

Keeping your slides simple, and ensuring they don't compete with your speech: these are key points, and it's here where most presenters go wrong. Remembering not to make this mistake is one of the most important takeaways from this book.

A client asked me to review a presentation she was putting together. Here's one of the bullets from a slide in her presentation:

- Given the effectiveness of normalizing data in a

snowflake schema, combined with an object-oriented relational database, you should be able to improve efficiency in designing and producing more useful financial reports by 50%.

I'm guessing that you feel the same way I did when I first read it: "Wow, this is a mouthful. There are many syllables, lots of words that aren't easy to process quickly...it's hard to follow." This kind of high-jargon language, displayed on the screen behind you, will compete with what you're saying while you are presenting.

You can make it much simpler and easier to comprehend. Here's one version that we came up with (there are other equally valid ones):

> Snowflake schema plus relational database
> means 50% faster reporting.

Simplifying the language does a lot to make the information more understandable. Ask yourself, what is the major point you are trying to make with each bit of data and what is the most concise way to phrase it? If you present your information in clear concise sound bites your audience's takeaway will be that much greater and won't compete with your speech.

Be sure to simplify any dense paragraphs, with lots of syllables and words that are hard to process. No one will be able to read that three line bullet and listen to you at the same time; simplify to one line instead.

For slides, less is often more. Aim for one point per slide. If you have 3 points in the slide, their "readability" is compromised. Split that one slide into three, one slide for each point. As an alternative, make use of "animation" if you have a complicated slide. Bring elements of the slide in one-by-one as you talk about them.

"And this section is profit from shipping and handling."

When we have expertise on a topic, we often tend to assume that people are going to understand what we are saying because they have some familiarity with the concepts we're presenting. Often, that is a false assumption, and it's commonly referred to as the *"curse of knowledge."* Understand your audience – where they are coming from and what they know. Do your best to put yourself in their place. Spell out clearly and concisely anything they might not know, without overwhelming them with complicated visuals. Ask yourself:

- Is there a simpler way for me to convey my point?
- Am I assuming too much about their knowledge?
- Will they understand this jargon?
- Will they know these acronyms?

I'll share with you a passage from an article in *The New York Times* by Adam Bryant, who writes a column called "*The Corner Office.*" For the column, he asks CEOs for examples of leadership in the workplace and what they look for in their employees. Bryant has compiled these interviews and his observations of the patterns they revealed. Here's an excerpt, as presented in the article ("*Distilling the Wisdom of C.E.O.'s,*" 4/16/2011):

There is a stubborn disconnect in many companies. Most senior executives want the same thing from people who present to them: be concise, get to the point, make it simple. Yet few people can deliver the simplicity that many bosses want. Instead, they mistakenly assume that the bosses will be impressed by a long PowerPoint presentation that shows how diligently they researched a topic, or that they will win over their superiors by talking more, not less.

Few things seem to get CEOs riled up more than lengthy PowerPoint presentations. It's not the software they dislike; that's just a tool. What irks them is the unfocused thinking that leads to overlong slide presentations. There is wide agreement that it's a problem: "death by PowerPoint" has become a cliché."

Take my advice, take Adam Bryant's advice, and keep your presentation and your slides really simple.

Chapter 4: Engaging

"Make sure you have finished speaking before your audience has finished listening."
Dorothy Sarnoff
(Famed Opera Soprano)

"I hear and I forget. I see and I remember. I do and I understand."
Confucius

4.1: Actively Engage Your Audience

Keep your audience interested by engaging them directly. You cannot assume that they're going to be focused on what you're saying. Maybe they are tired because the baby kept them up all night, or perhaps they're thinking about the last meeting they were in, or the next one. You have to do things to actively bring them into the present moment.

Ask questions: Involve your audience in the presentation! In a presentation skills training workshop, I often ask the audience "What is the key to a great presentation?" This gets them involved and thinking right from the start.

Questions can be as simple as: "How many of you have ever done 'x'?" Or "What do you do when 'y' happens?" For example, in a compensation negotiation presentation, I might ask the audience "What do you say when a prospect brings up cost when you are pitching your product to them?" Asking this question engages them and raises an issue of great interest!

Make sure the question you ask is relevant to the subject. Any random question will not do.

Engage Audience Directly
Ask them questions
Encourage dialogue/questions
Give Tests & Exercises
Use Surprise
Be creative!

Copyright 2013 Robert Hellmann - www.hellmannconsulting.com

Here's another example of using a question to engage the audience: A client was pitching his company's information services to a prospective corporate buyer. We created a slide that showed the logos of several well-known Fortune

500 companies and asked, "What do these companies all have in common?"

No one got the right answer, which was "They all use our services." My client not only engaged them by asking this question, but made an important point about his service's value. He ultimately got the sale.

Encourage dialogue/questions: I often say to the audience "Let's try to make this as much of a dialog as possible, so please feel free to ask questions."

Testing and Exercises: If you have a longer presentation, you might have time for exercises or quizzes. Substantial research has shown that testing is the most powerful way to help an audience (or yourself) retain information (more about the research on testing is in Chapter 9). You can throw in an impromptu pop quiz, like "True or False, the decision to buy is made within the first two minutes of your sales presentation." Get them going with a show of hands, or have them call out their answers. (The answer is "false" by the way; you have ample opportunity to turn a "no" into a "yes" based on what you do *after* the meeting. But that's for another book.)

Surprise: Using surprise (i.e. "shock value") is so effective that it gets its own letter in the *RESULTS* method! Be counter-intuitive, catch them off guard. Have them agree with a point you make and then say the point is wrong. Everything you want to know about using surprise in a presentation can be found in Chapter 9.

Be Creative: I attended an excellent product presentation about 15 years ago. I remember it vividly because the

presenter literally lit his product on fire! Now for obvious reasons, I'm not suggesting you light your presentation on fire. But use this example to inspire you to think outside the box.

"We're all very excited. Most of the other consultants do everything in a slide show presentation."

For example, I might throw out candy or chocolates or t-shirts to audience members who get a question right. Or perhaps give away books.

An attorney, presenting on legal regulations, created a game-show format quiz, split the room up into groups, and had them compete to answer questions about copyright law. The game format transformed a potentially boring topic into something fun and memorable. This presenter found a creative way to get the audience involved. Think of other ways you can get your audience involved, perhaps using a game format. To help you get started, two "game show" resources for presentations (I have no affiliation, these have been recommended by colleagues) include:

- Softworks "Bravo" at http://www.c3softworks.com/products/classroom/bravo-classroom/

- Learningware's "Gameshow Pro" at http://learningware.com/gameshowpro/index.html

Here's another creative approach: have the audience experience what you are advocating right in the room. **Experiential Learning** is a powerful way to help your audience retain information and understand your ideas. For example, in my "Peak Presentations" training classes, participants are asked to partner-up or form groups and try out the presentation and pitch techniques I'm sharing.

4.2 "HOOK" Them Early

Draw people in right from the start by having a really strong hook (and then reel them in with the rest of your presentation). Try one of these nine approaches to hooking your audience, all of which can be used anywhere in your presentation to great effect.

1. **Ask the Audience a Question**
   Any interesting, intelligent, relevant question posed to the audience at the start of your presentation can help hook the audience, since you are soliciting their active participation.

2. **Combine a Question with Surprise**
   Combining both of the above techniques is even more powerful. For example, sometimes in my organizational training workshops, I'll start off by asking the audience, as I did in Chapter 1, "Which of these five items is essential for a great presentation?" I'll list the five items that we described previously as "the mechanics." As I mentioned, no one ever gets the correct answer, which is "none of the above." And since people are surprised by the answer, they are immediately intrigued and want to know more.

3. **Use a Metaphor**
   Capturing the audience's imagination is a great way to engage them, and the visual imagery inherent in a metaphor helps to do that. For example, Sharon was putting together her pitch as part of a sales presentation for her company's "workflow management" software. Here is how she started her winning pitch: "A client once said to me 'our workflow was like the chaos of Manhattan streets

during rush hour. Your software transformed our process into a wide open superhighway.' As a matter of fact, we've helped many clients in your industry create their own workflow superhighways…"

4. **Tell a Short Story**

An engaging story can work wonders in any part of your presentation, and a short, bite-sized story at the start is no exception. As with the metaphor example, people will remember the story and therefore will be more likely to remember the point you are making as well.

For example, an Information Technology executive was presenting the case for investing in new system architecture. He started out his presentation with: "One morning last week, as I was walking to work, I saw someone trip on a broken piece of sidewalk in front of our building and fall! I ran over to help her; luckily, she was ok. As I think back to her dusting herself off and lamenting the crumbling infrastructure, I am reminded of the urgency with which we need to address not only our physical space, but our I.T. infrastructure problem before rolling out a new product…"

"Stories" gets its own letter in the *RESULTS* method as well; it's covered in detail in Chapter 5.

5. **State the Problem in Stark Terms**

   You can grab an audience's attention by simply stating the problem clearly and right up front. I learned this early in my career from a former manager. She would start her presentations by presenting the dilemma dramatically. For example, she might say something like "Competitor X is targeting our customers with product Y. We've already lost 5% of our customers over the past year, after 6 years of steady customer growth, and we have no solution." She didn't start off with the background, the research or a lengthy introduction. She simply got right to the point, with a problem or situation stated in dramatic terms that resonated with the audience. Her approach was always an attention-grabber.

6. **Leverage the News**

   For example, you might say "I'm sure you all heard the news that our stock price dropped this morning..." or "When I looked at the *Times* this morning the front page story was about our competitor." By bringing in the news, you are adding an immediacy and urgency to what you are about to say, in addition to bringing up a topic that may resonate with many in the audience.

7. **Make a Request or a Promise**

   With this approach, you are, by definition, directly engaging the audience. You might say something like: "When you leave this talk I promise that you will never think about our customers the same way again," or "I would like to request that later today, everybody take one suggestion that I made and see how you can apply it to your work situation."

8. **Use an Image**

   If it's the right image, you'll grab people's attention at the outset. For example, a fundraiser for a non-profit that provides aid for global emergencies displayed an image of a woman standing distraught amidst the devastation of the 2010 earthquake in Haiti. With one picture, the audience instantly got the message in a way that tugged at their emotions. This non-profit's mission is vitally important to millions of people. Engaging your audience's emotions is one of the most effective things you can do to make sure your presentation is memorable.

4.3 Using Visuals

Let's expand a bit on using images in your presentation. Pictures can be a great way to engage an audience. When used effectively, they add something new to the presentation that words can't communicate. When used ineffectively, they feel like a boring repetition of what has already been said, or worst case, they distract the audience from what you are saying. Let's look at a couple of examples.

Delivering Aid Globally

The picture shows a man and his son whose house was destroyed in the 2011 earthquake in Turkey.

This picture was shown in a non-profit's presentation to

foundations and large donors, in order to communicate the organization's mission and importance. Aid from the organization helped the family pictured to rebuild.

Here's another picture that the non-profit considered as an alternative, which also illustrates the concept of delivering aid globally.

Delivering Aid Globally

Which visual do you think is more effective for fundraising? Unanimously, people in my audiences have said the first visual, and I bet you're feeling the same way.

Two elements are present in the first picture, and not in the second that make the first picture more effective. First, you can see whom the aid is for. You're putting a face on an issue and providing the audience with a real person with whom they can connect. It's adding something to the presentation that's not there in the title.

In addition, you are engaging the audience's **emotions**. Extensive research has shown a close link between emotions and memory formation. People will understand why donating to this organization is so important, in a way that they might not from the second slide.

On the other hand, the visual on the second slide essentially repeats what's already in the title. It doesn't add anything new, nor does it engage emotions.

Let's take a look at another example. The slides that follow were part of an "enabling" presentation to inform the audience about how the brain works. In the next slide, you can see an illustration of the brain's complexity. The picture shows how the neurons in the brain are all interconnected.

The Brain is Complex

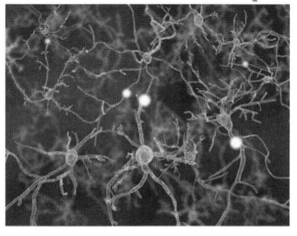

Now let's look at another version of this slide.

The Brain is Complex

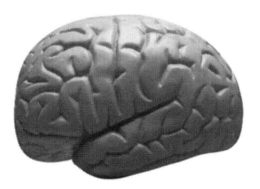

Which one do you like better? My guess is that you're going to choose the first one.

The first slide adds something new to the discussion by literally showing how complex the brain is. You can't get that just from the title or from an image of the outside of a brain.

When you're using visuals, strive to add something new to the presentation, whether it's an emotional tug, humor (which also engages emotions) or information that can't be conveyed as effectively with text alone.

Even if the visual doesn't add a lot, however, it can still aid in memory recall beyond just presenting text, as long as the visual is relevant and easy to comprehend. This *"Picture Superiority Effect"* has been well documented. From Wikipedia: *"The picture superiority effect refers to the notion that concepts that are learned by viewing pictures are more easily and frequently recalled than are concepts that are learned by viewing their written word form counterparts. This effect has been demonstrated in numerous experiments using different methods."* Google the phrase, and you will find pages of entries discussing this effect and the research behind it.

Here is an example of how this effect works in practice. One client was giving a presentation on the latest research showing the relationship between wolves and dogs. One of her slides contained the following text:

- **Dogs may have evolved from wolves in just a few generations**

To improve retention of this idea, we created the following slide:

Just a few generations from...

 to

Notice that we could have shown just the pictures without text, and had my client make the point by talking over the slide. Research has shown, however, that simple text combined with a visual is even more effective for audience retention than just showing the visual-- which in turn is more effective than just showing the text.

4.4 Challenging Audience Interactions

Sometimes you'll run into a situation where people are a bit over-engaged - a questioner goes on too long, or someone is rude or off-topic. Or maybe a senior executive challenges you in a way that leaves you feeling defensive or unprepared. How do you handle these situations?

Someone Goes On Too Long

This kind of annoyance is business as usual if you give a lot of presentations. People frequently ask questions that take up too much time. You usually know what they're asking 10 minutes before they're done speaking. How do you handle this?

Start by thinking about the bigger picture. The rest of the audience really wants to hear your presentation, and doesn't want to sit through their long question either.

If you're thinking about the greater good, then the ideal thing for you to do is to interrupt them politely and apologetically, but firmly. Mention the limited time. Say something like, "I'm sorry, I think I know where you're going with this. Just in the interest of time, let me paraphrase. You're asking X right?" They'll say, "Yes." Then you'll answer the question.

Rudeness

Hopefully you won't get rude questions or comments when you present, but the occasional rude outburst does occur. The key is to think once again about the greater good, the desire of the larger audience to hear what you came to say. To ensure that the needs of the many are met, you need to manage the rude audience member politely, but firmly. Take the high road, and then steer the discussion back to what you want to talk about.

Here's a personal example. Years ago, I was giving a talk at the Department of Labor. It was going well. I had delivered this talk many times, with excellent results. The audience was positively engaged, and I knew that the talk was being well-received. In the midst of a brief pause for questions, an audience member suddenly shot up out of his seat and loudly said, "Can we please get on with the presentation?"

Instead of getting upset or defensive, I simply said, "Don't worry. Everything is fine. We're right on schedule," and then I turned it back to my agenda, as if his interruption never happened.

Surprisingly (or maybe not so surprisingly), after the event was over, this rude person acted like he wanted to be my best friend. He thanked me profusely and later emailed to say how much he enjoyed the presentation. He kept in

touch with me to update me about his career,
stood up to him politely but firmly and steere
my agenda.

The moral of the story: You don't want to derail the presentation because of someone's rudeness, nor do you want to respond with rudeness. If necessary, you can address the individual one-on-one after the presentation is over.

A classic example of how to handle a rude questioner involves Steve Jobs and is available on YouTube. Google *"Steve Jobs Insult Response"* (or copy the link shown in Appendix B) to find the video. He takes the high road, ignores the insult and uses the rude question as an opportunity to segue back to what he had come to share with the audience.

Off-topic Questions or Comments

Audience members frequently raise off-topic points. Just recently, I was delivering a presentation and an audience member asked a question that was a complete digression.

This was a prime time for me to think about the needs of the larger audience. Here's what I said: "Listen, that's a bit off-topic. I want to answer that question. I think it's a great question, but let's address it at the end of the meeting or

..er the meeting. Come and ask me about it or e-mail me and we can set up a time to talk."

Another option is to answer even more briefly. For example, say "The answer is Yes (or No) but since that's a different topic, why don't we talk about it further after the meeting? Or you can send me an e-mail to set up an appointment to discuss it."

Also, keep in mind that the person raising the question may not realize that there is not enough time available to answer, so a simple, polite response from you is ideal.

Audience Members Talking While You're Presenting
Often, a couple of people may still be talking with each other while you are starting to present. This usually happens right after a break or a group activity. In this case, thinking about the needs of the larger audience means that others may not be able to hear you over the conversation. Say politely, "Sorry, excuse me. I just want to make sure the others can hear me." They'll stop. No problem. Very easy.

Someone Strongly Challenges You
If someone strongly challenges your key point, you may suddenly feel defensive. This often happens when you're

presenting to more senior people or when you are presenting to academics, specialists or other experts.

Instead of leaping to the defense of your point, first understand why they are challenging you. They might say something like, "I don't agree at all with those assumptions," or, "I think your product idea will never work." You've got to find out why they are questioning your key point in order to address their comment.

"Better let me lead off the presentation."

Give yourself time to think of a response by repeating or paraphrasing the question that they just asked. Paraphrasing will also ensure that you fully understand their comment or question.

Ultimately, you'll want to say, "While I understand your point, here's why I see it a bit differently." Make sure you are polite, but that you stand up for your point of view.

Let me give you an example from personal experience. I interviewed for a position many years ago and I met a number of wonderful people throughout the process.

However, when I met the last person, the most senior person, my boss' boss, we immediately got off on the wrong foot. He started the interview by saying, "I think you want too much money and I don't think you're qualified for the position." Not even a handshake or a "Hi, how are you!"

I asked him, "Why do you say that?" I needed more information. He told me his reasons. Then I said, "I understand your point; I do see it in a different way, however…" and then I calmly laid out my case.

Ultimately, I did get the offer, after an apology from him. He said he was just testing me because the organization had some difficult clients and he wanted to make sure I'd be able to handle them.

Lastly, you can always say, "That's a really great point. I hadn't thought of that," or, "I don't know the answer. I'll get back to you." In fact, saying "I don't know" can add to your overall credibility (as long as you don't say it too often) since your honesty about your lack of knowledge makes you more believable when you say you do know something.

By the way, if the interaction starts to go back and forth between you and the challenger and feels a bit out of control, you can always say, "Why don't we continue this discussion after the presentation?" That way, your entire talk won't be disrupted.

Chapter 5: Stories

"We love to hear stories. We don't need another lecture. Just ask your kids."
George Torok
(motivational speaker)

"Great stories don't appeal to logic, but they often appeal to our senses."
Seth Godin

The next element in the *RESULTS* method involves telling stories. Incorporating a great story into your delivery is the fastest way to improve your presentation.

I observed a presentation where the speaker was subpar; he possessed a disheveled appearance, a monotone voice, and dense over-complicated slides that competed with what he was saying. His goal was to get his audience interested in paying him to learn how to coach using emotional intelligence, and he was failing.

He did one thing very right, however; he told two great stories, which is the reason I still remember him today. One story in particular stayed with me. He used it to illustrate how his approach to emotional intelligence works.

He spoke of his client, who although she was considered

very sharp by her boss and work colleagues, was close to being fired. In 360 reviews and other feedback, she was variously described as demanding, inappropriate, unpleasant, rude, disruptive and a host of other unflattering adjectives. Her colleagues simply didn't like working with her.

She could have easily been fired, but her bosses decided to give her one more chance by having her work with this consultant. He described taking her through a number of exercises that made clear to her how her lack of "emotional intelligence" was hurting her at work.

She developed a new awareness of the impact of her difficult personal style. The consultant was then able to use exercises with her to build up her emotional intelligence. In the process, her colleagues' perception of her changed completely, and later reviews were much more positive. The result: she went from being nearly fired to becoming a star in the space of a year.

With this story (and a similar one that he shared) the speaker transformed a mediocre presentation into something powerful and memorable. The result for him was that several people signed up for his training program because they recognized the value of coaching emotional intelligence. Plus, he was invited back to speak again to the group.

Now, let's review what I just did; I shared with you a story to illustrate the power of storytelling in a presentation. I laid out the story in a particular format. I started off with the problem, which in this case was that he was a poor presenter who was failing in reaching his objective. Then I described the action he took, which was to tell two great stories. Then I let you know the result, which was that he got people to sign on to his approach and he received another speaking engagement.

This PAR format - problem, action, result - is something you should incorporate in your own stories.

Give Examples using PAR   Stories

1. **P**roblem/Situation
2. **A**ction
3. **R**esult

When you talk about the problem, be sure to tie it to the bottom line. The bottom line could be time, money, happiness, whatever really matters to the audience. Then talk about the steps you took to solve the problem. Conclude with the result, by tying it back again to the bottom line. In a business setting, if you can tie the story to dollars, opportunity cost, money saved, market share, or other clear business metrics, you will get their attention.

Some people have trouble understanding what I mean by the bottom line. In the story I just told you, the bottom line was that the presenter wasn't going to get what he wanted, that is, audience members who would buy his training approach. In the story he told, the bottom line was that the person with emotional intelligence issues was on the verge of being fired.

When you're using stories to illustrate a point, try to make them **dramatic, engaging and emotional!** Pretend you're trying to hold the attention of a 5-year-old. People are busy. They have limited attention spans. You have to make your presentation interesting and engaging, while being neither too simple, nor too detailed, nor too high-level. It's got to be right in the middle.

To go back to the story I shared about the poor presenter, I added dramatic, descriptive details to hold your interest. For example, I shared all the negative adjectives that work colleagues used when referring to the executive. This creates stakes and a clear sense of the obstacle she faced.

Here's another example. A client was making his case for creating a new hire onboarding process at his company (i.e. a process for quickly and productively integrating new hires into the organization), a process that would require a significant investment. Here's the story he told to get executive buy-in on the investment he was seeking.

"Where I used to work, we did something similar to what I'm proposing. Let me share with you what we did because I think we can replicate it here. At my prior company <his new company's competitor> we figured out we were losing about a million dollars a year because we were not ready for new hires. The desks weren't there, the laptops and the PCs weren't there. New hires didn't know where to go, who to talk to. They didn't even understand the basic acronyms that the company used every day. It was a problem and it was costing us a lot of money.

Here's what we did. I contacted facilities. I set up an arrangement with them to ensure that we would have cubicles and desks ready for new hires by their first day. I talked to IT. We setup an arrangement where a laptop or a PC would be available for the new hires the day they arrived. We set up some online training and some in-class training so new hires would become familiar with the key acronyms, the key processes, the operations of the departments and the company. We even assigned each new executive hire a "mentor" to guide them through the period of orientation.

Based on manager surveys and the feedback from the new hires, this program was a great success. The bottom line for my prior company was that, for $25,000 worth of salaries they needed to spend to make this happen, they figured they were saving about a million dollars a year with the new onboarding process. We could do the same thing here."

In my client's example, the problem was made more dramatic by tying it to the bottom line, i.e. losing roughly $1 million a year, and then solving the problem with just a $25,000 investment. In addition, he made an effort to dramatize the story by adding interesting details, such as *"The desks weren't there, the laptops or the PC's weren't there…I contacted facilities…"*

This story was key to my client getting his proposal approved. Do you see how giving this example brought his onboarding proposal to life? If he just laid-out the proposal without the example, the presentation wouldn't have been nearly as strong.

I hope you'll notice that I've told many stories and given examples to help illustrate the points I've been making throughout this book. If you listen to Steve Jobs' Stanford Commencement Speech (Appendix B), you will see that it's effective because he told three dramatic, engaging emotional stories. The power of those stories is what makes his speech such an oratorical classic.

Chapter 6: Useful

"Good communication, written or oral, begins with an understanding of the audience. If you can get inside their heads, you can find a way to connect."
Debra Bennetts
(Marketing and PR Expert)

When you evaluate a speaker you've just heard, you may ask yourself, "What did I get out of this talk?" or "What's my take-away?" Your audience members are thinking the same thing about your presentation. Everyone wants to know "How does this help me?"

When you're making your presentation, this is the number one question you need to address. Focus on your audience's bottom line, whether it's time, money, happiness, market share, efficiency or something else.

In some cases, you can even refer to people in the audience and say something like "and Steve, this will help your department because…" or "Each of you need to know this because…"

In the world of work, the name of the game is solving problems. If you can solve other peoples' problems (your boss's, client's, prospect's, etc.) you will be successful.

But don't make the common mistake of confusing the "features and benefits" of your own product, service or idea with the "problems" you can solve for the audience. Keep your presentation focused on *their* needs. Otherwise it will be too much about you and not enough about them.

I worked with a colleague who developed client relationship management (CRM) software. I used his product and, finding it useful, connected him with a business owner who I felt could make use of the software. I was invited to their initial meeting.

My colleague started his pitch by talking about his product. About 5 minutes or so into his presentation, I suspected he was not going to get the sale, and sure enough, he didn't.

Why? Because he kept talking about this or that feature and benefit of his software. He should have focused instead on the challenges the small business owner was facing. He should have asked, "What are you doing around CRM right now? How are you set up for CRM? What's the biggest problem you're facing? Have you ever thought about this? Have you ever thought about that?" Then he would have been able to pitch his CRM software within the context of their problems and issues.

We ended up rewriting his pitch, resulting in much more success. You can read his revised pitch in Chapter 10, page 76.

One last example: In an organization with which I was involved, the President had a habit of asking presenters, "So, what do we do with this information?" Too many had no answer. One even said "That's a great question, I'm not sure." NOT a good answer!

Be ready to clearly describe how what you are presenting will help your audience. Put yourself in your audience's shoes; that should help to keep you on track.

Chapter 7: Licensed

*"It takes many good deeds to build a good reputation,
and one bad one to lose it."*
Benjamin Franklin

You need to be "licensed" to deliver the material in your presentation. This means having the credentials, experience and results to be considered believable by your audience. You've got to make your case.

I did that, by the way, in this book's Introduction and the "About the Author" section by talking about my background and experience. You've got to do that as well.

Sometimes it's easy. Perhaps you have a reputation in the industry, or you were referred by someone who's trusted and already "licensed." You can also become "licensed" by simply saying "I spent the last 3 months researching X, Y, and Z, and here are my results." Your three months of research establishes your authority.

Sometimes it's not so easy. Maybe your audience sees you as an outsider and they are consequently skeptical of anything you share with them. This might be the situation if you are presenting to a very technical audience, e.g. scientists, statisticians, economists etc. and you don't have a similar professional background. With this type of audience, you must make an extra effort to gain their respect and be taken seriously. The best way to do so is to share something that shows you "get" them.

For example, I sometimes deliver presentation skills seminars to scientists and researchers who are new to the business world. They tend to share highly technical, research-based information without the recommendations or point of view that would make it useful to a profit-driven organization. Perhaps they got used to presenting like this within their university setting.

To help these presenters understand the differences between the academic and business worlds, I do two things: a) chat with audience members before the presentation and incorporate details about their jobs or the business scenarios they encounter into the speech; b) use phrasing in the presentation such as, "You're probably thinking that you can do "x"- making sure to say something that will get the audience nodding their heads in agreement. Then I tell them what they really need to be doing!

The point is, you must establish your "license" to deliver your presentation effectively. Not doing so can undermine the success of your entire presentation, even if you are doing everything else right. No one will care much for what you say if you don't convince them up front of your expertise and authority.

Chapter 8: Tailored

"No one ever complains about a speech being too short!"
Ira Hayes
(Flag Raiser at Iwo Jima)

"Much speech is one thing, well-timed speech is another."
Sophocles

"Tailored" is about managing audience expectations. You need to tailor your presentation by knowing who will be in your audience and what they expect. Do your research! Ask people who've presented to this audience before or ask audience members directly before the presentation.

"She has a 2:42 and a 2:43 appointment. I can try to fit you in."

Sometimes clients say, "How do I ask the audience beforehand?" If you are presenting to an executive, you can try stopping by their office for 5 minutes and just say, "Hi, I'm on your calendar in a couple of weeks. I want to make sure I understand your expectations. Do you want me to give you an overview of our department or what our process is, or would you like me to help you to make a specific decision?" The key point is that you don't want to go in there thinking they want X when they really want Y.

8.1 Process-Oriented vs. "Tell Me Now"

One of the ways you can think about your audience is to understand whether they are process-oriented or "tell me now" types. Process-oriented means they want to hear the steps you took to reach your conclusions before hearing the conclusion. "Tell me now" means "just give me your bottom line conclusion, and then we'll talk about the steps, if we need to."

Approximately two-thirds of senior executives fall into the "tell me now" category. They are impatient and want to know the bottom line right away. The other third are more process-oriented. If you can get a sense of that ahead of time, it's going to help you organize your presentation to meet their expectations.

Sometimes you will have a combination of types in the audience. In that case, compromise. You put an executive summary up-front, or a teaser, "Here's where we're going with this," then go into the steps.

At the start of my career, I learned the importance of tailoring a presentation to the audience the hard way. I had produced a number of charts and tables to help show the steps and process leading to my conclusion. I thought the senior executive I was meeting with would be impressed, but it turned out he wanted to get right to the point. "Just tell me what to do," he said.

Let's take this analysis of audience expectations a step further. You want to anticipate the questions in which they are most interested. Questions usually focus on:

Ideas: "Did you think about trying this or that?"

Steps Involved: "What do we need to get this done?"

People: "Who is this going to impact?"

Understanding: "How did you arrive at your conclusion?"

In fact, individuals may tend to care more about one of these four groups of questions than the remaining three; your presentation planning will be more effective if you know in advance what types of questions your audience tends to focus on. For example, one of my former bosses, more than anyone else I have worked for, always went to the "people impact" of any idea first, before getting to the steps or other questions. For another, the people impact was more of an afterthought—for her it was all about "how," much less about "who"!

8.2 The "1/3rd" Rule

Here's another way of thinking about tailoring your speech. Let's say you have an hour to do an important presentation to a senior executive. Do you bring an hour's worth of slides and material? No, bring maybe a third of that, roughly 20 minutes.

This "1/3 rule" arises because usually your client can't (or doesn't want to) give the full time allotted on her/his calendar to your presentation. S/he may be coming in late from another meeting, or needs to leave early or has questions and wants to take the presentation in a different direction. That's typically how it goes when you're presenting to senior people.

If you have 30 minutes to present, you should prepare 10 minutes of slides and material. If you have one hour, present 20 minutes of slides and material. This way you're not trying to force the executive to look at a lot of slides and data for which they don't have the time or interest. It also forces you to prioritize what's really important and boil your message down to its concise, powerful essence.

Be ready with additional material to share should the executive want to make use of the additional two thirds of the time that's allotted. Create maximum flexibility to take the conversation in different directions. Bring additional charts, tables and ideas that you can share with them if you have more time, but don't go in assuming you'll have the full hour scheduled.

Above all, don't try to force the executive to hear all the material you brought along with you. That's not tailoring your presentation to your audience and could result in a frustrated executive.

By the way, the 1/3rd rule covers situations where you're meeting with an executive or a couple of executives. The rule does not apply to more formal presentations where the attendees have signed up and expect to have an hour of material presented. In the case of the smaller meeting with one or a few executives, they'll be grateful for time back on their calendar if the presentation ends up being shorter than the time they allotted.

Chapter 12 contains suggestions for organizing your presentation in both more formal and informal settings.

Chapter 9: Surprising

"When you advertise fire extinguishers,
open with the fire."
David Ogilvy

Bring surprise into your presentation to make it memorable and powerful. Humans evolved to remember the unusual, the shocking, something that breaks from the routine. Use this knowledge to your benefit.

We started one client's presentation (to an executive audience at a Fortune 500 company) with a slide that had a single large number on it. Then he said:

> *"3 million dollars. That's right. 3 million dollars. That's how much our company loses every year due to retraining, and the cost of hiring new employees, because of our high attrition rate. But we can cut that number in half for a one-time $100,000 investment."*

My client reported back to me that the audience was surprised all around by both the magnitude of the cost and the inexpensive fix. In short, they were paying rapt attention right from the beginning — they wanted to know more, and my client had them "hooked."

$3,000,000

Here's another example of using surprise to engage your audience. In my presentation skills workshops, I'll often display the following slide and I'll ask the audience, "Which of these methods listed on the screen is most effective in getting students to retain information that's presented to them? Studying, testing without any studying, a visual mapping exercise where the points in the passage are visually mapped onto a piece of paper, doing nothing or it doesn't matter?" Most of the audience will pick the visual mapping exercise, and a significant number will pick studying alone. Every so often, someone will say testing.

Which information retention method works best?

1. Studying
2. Test
3. Visual Mapping Exercise
4. Doing nothing
5. All the same

Copyright 2013 Robert Hellmann - www.hellmannconsulting.com

When I tell them that according to a study published in the journal *Science* (Feb. 11, 2011), the answer is actually "testing," most of the audience is surprised. In fact, testing is 50% more effective than studying or visual mapping! For my audiences, this tends to be one of the more memorable parts of the training.

Notice that I opened this book with a surprising revelation. I showed the slide asking "What is key to a great presentation?" and the surprising answer was "None-of-the above." I did this to get you more interested in what I was about to say than if I had simply stated the keys to a great presentation.

Here's another example. When I deliver a presentation on interviewing, I will put up a slide that says "The hiring decision is made within the first two minutes of the interview." I then ask the audience what they think of this statement. Most of them agree with it. Then I surprise them by telling them that this is absolutely false, that there is ample opportunity to turn a "no" into a "yes" based on what you do even after the interview is over! Now they are both surprised and intrigued; they want to know more.

One final example from this same presentation on Interviewing; it illustrates well how you can engage the audience by bringing up something that's counter-intuitive, or even shocking. I ask the audience "How many of you write 'thank you' letters?" Almost everyone raises their hands. Then I say "OK, from now on, no more thank you letters." The audience is always surprised, shocked even. That can't be right! I pause for a couple of seconds, then say, "I want you to write '*influence* letters," and then I explain what I mean by that. They are riveted.

Chapter 10: *RESULTS* & Your Pitch

A wise man speaks because he has something to say, a fool speaks because he has to say something."
Plato

Chapters 3 through 9 covered how to apply each element of the *RESULTS* method to your influencing or enabling presentation. In Chapter 10, we'll cover situations where you need to deliver a presentation in two minutes or less.

Your "pitch" is a mini-presentation that can last anywhere from five seconds to two minutes, depending on the situation. The goal of the pitch is to present yourself in a way that gets people interested and wanting to hear more. It's used in business development, sales, networking, informational meetings and interviews.

In this chapter, we are going to cover how to:

- Organize your pitch
- Adapt your pitch to different situations
- Incorporate *RESULTS* into your pitch to make it shine.

YOUR PITCH
Two Minute
30 Second
15 Second
5 Second

The length of your pitch will differ depending on the situation.

At work you should have a **5-second pitch** ready to go in case you get an unexpected visit from your boss, or to take advantage of meeting situations where the dialogue gives you an opportunity to showcase something you've done.

When you're leaving a voice message or talking to an administrative assistant, you'll have a very limited amount of time, maybe 15 or 20 seconds, before they lose interest. That's when you need a **15-second pitch**.

A **30-second pitch** is for networking situations or sales encounters, when you'll have a bit more time.

A **two-minute pitch** can be used when you're delivering a formal sales presentation, when you're in an interview and they ask you "tell me about yourself," or when you are in an informational meeting and you introduce yourself or remind them of your background.

Five elements comprise the pitch. For anything less than a 30 second pitch, you'll only be able to use a subset of the five.

Here is a chart with the five elements listed and mapped to the different pitch lengths.

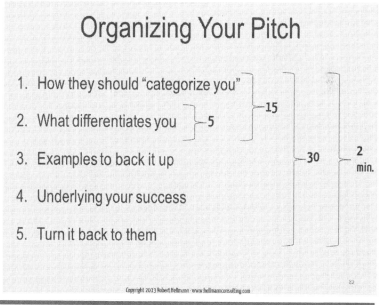

- **How should they "categorize" you, and why they should care:** Tell them how they should think about you, what "box" to place you in. "Marketing expert" is an example. If time allows, add something about why they should pay attention, for example "…I believe marketing starts with listening to your customers…"

- **What differentiates you:** Let them know what makes you interesting. How do you stand out from others in the same category? For example, "I'm a marketing executive…" is the category, and "…with particular expertise in Latin American markets and social media."

- **Examples to back it up:** Give a couple of examples to back up your claim about what category you're in and what makes you different from others they've heard from before. Share high-level accomplishment-oriented examples. "For example, we did x which resulted in y."

- **Underlying your success:** Tell people what makes you successful. For example, "Our success has been based on our ability to customize our product to the needs of each of our clients."

- **Turn it back to them:** Remember to keep the focus on where your audience is coming from and how you can address their needs. For example, you can end with "...and I'm excited to be talking with you because I have read a lot about your move into this new customer segment and I wanted to ask you about it..."

For shorter pitches, there isn't enough time to bring in all five elements. If you're giving a 5-second pitch, you will only have time to focus on how you differ from others. If you are giving a 15-second pitch, you'll have time for both how they should categorize you and how you are different. For a 30-second or two-minute pitch, you'll have time for all 5 elements. Let's dive into some examples.

10.1 Five Seconds

A 5-second pitch can really come in handy in work situations. You can use it when your boss (or any higher up) comes by unexpectedly, so you have something to say that will impress them if they inquire about how things are going. Similarly, in meetings, you may find an opportunity to share your 5-second pitch, depending on the conversation.

For example, Julie was in an elevator at work. The doors opened and in walked her boss's boss's boss, who she hardly ever saw. This senior person said to my client, "Hi,

Julie. How are you doing?"

Julie could have simply said, "Fine. How about you?" Instead, because we had put together a 5-second pitch for her, she said, "Things are great, now that I've just completed the workflow management project." The senior executive said, "I had no idea you were involved with that. Tell me about it."

She said, "Well, it's been a great success. We're about to roll it out." This resulted in a discussion about the workflow project. The senior person ended the discussion by saying, "Now that I know about your leadership role with this project, I think you should be involved in the cross-department workflow redesign project that I'm about to initiate. I'm going to talk to your boss about it."

By sharing her 5-second pitch during this unexpected encounter, Julie transformed what could have been a mundane interaction into something that gave her career a boost. She was now on the radar of this very senior person and was even being considered for an important project.

How was the *RESULTS* method used to craft this 5-second pitch, so that Julie could achieve her objectives? First off, she kept **Really Simple** in mind. She made sure that the executive would get the concept she was sharing immediately. There was no jargon involved that the executive wouldn't understand.

Julie also kept in mind that she wanted to make it **Useful** for the executive. She shared something that the executive would want to know.

Lastly, she **Tailored** the pitch to the situation. She knew she would have a very limited amount of time to deliver it so she ensured that she generated interest in her accomplishment in 5 seconds.

10.2 15 Seconds

Sometimes you have only 15 or 20 seconds to get your

---

message across. Maybe you need to leave a voice message with someone you don't know. Or, perhaps you are making a cold-call and you have to grab their attention quickly.

In these cases, you want to use your 15-second pitch. In 15 seconds, you will have time to bring in 2 elements of the pitch:

- How they should categorize you
- What differentiates you

My client, Susan, is a tax expert and legal counsel who is on the business development side of things. She was trying to get a meeting with someone who might be interested in her services. This is the message that Susan left:

"Hi, this is Susan Smith. I sent you an e-mail earlier this week. I'm a tax expert and counsel with specific experience in Latin America and, in particular, Brazil, where I know you're expanding. Can we set up a 20-minute call for a mutually beneficial conversation? My number is 555-555-5555. I'll try your office again as well, as I may be hard to reach."

In 15 to 20 seconds, Susan was able to bring in both how they should categorize her ("I am a tax expert and counsel") and how she differs from other callers ("experience in Latin America and, in particular, Brazil, where I know you're expanding").

How did the *RESULTS* method help to make her 15-second pitch more powerful? First, she kept the message **Really Simple**. She said nothing that would require the recipient to have to listen to the message again to catch something they missed (unless they want to catch the phone number again).

Really Simple

Engaging

Stories

Useful

Licensed

Tailored

Surprising

15 Second Pitch

She also **Engaged** the listener by asking a question: "Can we set up a 20-minute call?" She made it **Useful** by mentioning how she could help. She **Tailored** it by keeping in mind the 15-second time frame and mentioned that she knew about their expansion. In other words, she focused on them and their needs. Lastly, she indicated that she was **Licensed** to provide this help by mentioning her experience.

10.3 Two Minutes

Now let's address situations where you'll have a little bit more time, say 30 seconds or two minutes. We'll actually discuss pitching yourself in two minutes because the 30-second version is just a shorter version, and both contain all five pitch elements. Take two minutes to pitch yourself in these situations:

- You're in a business development meeting and have time to present yourself and your product or services.
- You're in an informational meeting (for example, you landed a meeting with someone in an industry different from yours, so you can learn more about that industry), and you start off by reminding the listener of your background and how you can help an organization.
- You're in an interview and they ask you open-ended questions such as "Tell me about yourself" (If you are interested in reading more about how to apply "The Two Minute Pitch" specifically to job-search interviewing, the Five O'Clock Club has an

excellent, in-depth discussion of the topic in their book *Mastering the Job Interview and Winning the Money Game* by Kate Wendleton).

Earlier in the book I mentioned a colleague who had developed customer relationship management (CRM) software, but his pitch to a small business owner failed. Here's the improved pitch we created, which brought in great results:

"Imagine a world where prospects welcome your emails and outreach; where building meaningful, profitable, win-win dialogue with prospects and customers is simple and easy. Our clients tell us we've built such a world for them with our CRM solution, and we welcome you to it!

We've helped dozens of companies in your industry save time, money, and improve revenue with our flagship product. Our system covers all aspects of CRM from X to Y to Z. It's hosted both in the cloud and on your servers so your data is always secure. Let me share with you an example so you can get a better idea of how we can help you.

We were hired by a major Fortune 500 company to deliver our CRM solution. Following their implementation of our system, in that first year alone they saw a 60% drop in customer service issues and a 30% reduction in staff hours devoted to CRM. This translated into savings in the millions for them.

We won an award from Workflow Today Magazine for the best tool for small to mid-sized companies. We've been featured as the standard to beat in CRM Weekly. We also have 40 verifiable testimonials on our company page, many from well-known companies such as X, Y, and Z. You may want to take a look at those.

Underlying our success, I believe, has been our ability to customize solutions to the needs of individual companies, departments, and even users. I'm excited to be talking with you about this because I understand from Marc that you're facing this and that issue. I think those issues are directly addressed by our service."

That was the pitch. Let's talk about how each of the five elements were incorporated.

- **How they should "categorize" you/Why they should care:** He mentioned, at the beginning, *"Imagine a world where prospects welcome your emails and outreach; where building meaningful, profitable, win-win dialogue with prospects and customers is simple and easy. Our clients tell us that we've built such a world for them with our CRM solution, and we would like to welcome you to it."*

- **What differentiates you:** He brought in what

makes his system different from competitors. *"In fact, our system covers all aspects of CRM from X to Y to Z. It's hosted both in the cloud and on your servers so your data is always secure."*

- **Examples to back it up:** He mentioned the reduction in customer services issues, articles in magazines, testimonials and so forth.

- **Tie it all together:** He said *"Underlying our success, I believe, has been our ability to customize solutions to the needs of individual companies, department, and even users."*

- **Turn it back to them:** He ended with: *"I'm excited to be talking with you about this because I understand from Marc that you're facing this and that issue. I think those issues are directly addressed by our service."* He resumed the focus on their problems and their issues.

In this 2-minute pitch, my colleague was able to incorporate almost all aspects of the *RESULTS* method, everything except for **Surprising.**

Really Simple

Engaging

Stories

Useful

Licensed

Tailored

Surprising

Two Minute Pitch

First off, he kept it **Really Simple**. No jargon, very easy to understand.

He used a powerful "hook" (see Chapter 4) to directly **Engage** the audience right at the beginning. He invited the audience to imagine their ideal prospecting world, then linked that world to their CRM product, and finally "invited" them to join this world.

This type of hook works very well, by the way, when you are pitching a product or service. Instead of starting off with WHAT your product is, start off with the WHY, i.e. what you *believe the world could be like*. Then invite your listeners to join you in this belief. Taking this approach encourages an emotional response, which is always helpful in making your presentation powerful and memorable.

He told a **Story**. Of course, it was abbreviated, given the time frame, but the example he shared was essentially a mini-story.

His message was focused on how his software company could be **Useful** in helping this small business owner with their client relationship management issues. Throughout the pitch, he used the word "you" as in "we welcome you...," "how we can help you..." and so forth, to drive home the relevance of their product to this audience.

For **Licensed**, he shared his testimonials, how they'd helped dozens of companies and how they were featured in a prestigious industry publication.

Lastly, he **Tailored** his pitch to fit into the short timeframe. He also talked about how he could customize the CRM solution to their individual needs. At the end, he focused the conversation back to them, talking about how he understood what their issues were and how he thought he could offer them a solution.

Chapter 11: Managing Anxiety

There are only two types of speakers in the world.
1. The nervous and 2. Liars
Mark Twain

"The human brain starts working the moment you are born
and never stops, until you stand up to speak in public."
George Jessel

I'm currently delivering roughly 100 presentations a year to audiences of diverse sizes and backgrounds. As much as I enjoy the experience of sharing knowledge and inspiring and influencing people, I still get nervous from time to time. In particular, I feel slightly nervous when the material I'm presenting is newer and I'm less comfortable with it. The more I've practiced a certain presentation, the more I know what's coming, and the less nervous I am.

You need to practice and memorize as much of your presentation as possible. For long presentations, memorizing word for word may not be practical. But if you tend to get nervous, memorizing at least the beginning will help a lot, since that's when people tend to feel the most nervous.

Also, you want to be sure you are not surprised by unexpected events. That starts with your slides! Make sure you know what's coming up. I like to print out six slides per page and place them on a table right where I'm presenting. Every so often I'll glance at them just to remind myself of the slides that are coming up next. I'll also make notes on the slides I've printed when I feel it's useful. Here's an example.

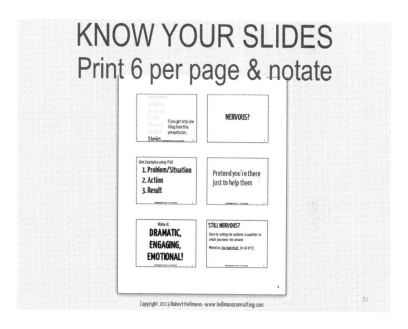

Steve Jobs was known to rehearse for days and hours on end to ensure that his presentations went off without a hitch.

For many, however, all the preparing in the world won't alleviate the anxiety that comes with standing in front of a large group of people. If you fall into this category, here are some techniques that may help.

Presentations make me nervous

Pretend that you're there just to help them
Train your mind to think that you have already gotten what you want. Your presentation is not going to get you that promotion, approval, job or sale, because you already have it. You're on the same side of the table as they are, looking to help them. If you can pretend you have already gotten what you want, you will not be as nervous because you won't feel as though you have as much on the line. In addition, you will be naturally focused on answering every audience member's number one question: "How does this help me?"

Ask the Audience a Question
At the beginning of your presentation (when you are most nervous), start by asking the audience a relevant question to which you know the answer. While you are calling on people in the audience to answer the question, two things are happening: 1) You have established yourself as the

"authority" (not only to the audience, but subconsciously to yourself as well), and 2) You've given yourself time to calm down and relax; you already know the answer, yet you are watching them struggle to find it. It's an easy way for you to quickly feel more confident right at the start, which is often the most anxiety-producing part of the presentation.

Visualize the Presentation

Find a conference room, or go to your office, bathroom, etc., close the door, and shut your eyes. Then run through all the steps of the presentation in your mind. Imagine hearing yourself introduced, then stepping up to the front of the room, seeing the audience, starting your presentation, hearing a question from the audience and responding to it and so on. Visualize every step. Going through this mental exercise is a powerful dress rehearsal that will make you feel much calmer during the actual event. I've done this for high-pressure situations and it works well!

Breathe

The next time you feel nervous before a presentation, try this: Slowly breathe in, then slowly breathe out. While doing so, try to focus completely on your breath moving in and out. Picture the air being drawn into your lungs and then flowing out. Repeat this five times, or as many times as it takes until you are totally focused on your breathing.

If you are totally focused on your breathing, by definition you cannot be nervous. Anxiety is worry about the future. With this breathing exercise, you have transferred your focus from the future to the present. This change in focus breaks the spell of anxiety. Even a temporary break, through this breathing exercise, is often enough to diminish your overall anxiety level.

"Fake it Until You Become It" (as per Amy Cuddy)
You can feel more confident simply by physically acting more confident, according to research. Just as the act of smiling, without any outside stimulus, can make you feel happier, standing or sitting in a confident, assertive way can reduce your anxiety. Try it yourself: take two minutes prior to a meeting, go someplace private and practice standing with your hands on your hips, or with your arms way out, like you are trying to make yourself bigger. Doing these exercises should take the edge off of your anxiety.

To learn more about the approach I'm suggesting, I highly recommend that you review the research conducted by Amy Cuddy at Harvard, as described in the New York Times (*"Amy Cuddy Takes a Stand,"* September 19th 2014) and in her TED Talk:
(http://www.ted.com/talks/amy_cuddy_your_body_langu age_shapes_who_you_are).

Chapter 12: Organizing your Presentation

"A place for everything and everything in its place."
Benjamin Franklin

"First comes thought; then organization of that thought into ideas and plans; then transformation of those plans into reality. The beginning, as you will observe, is in your imagination."
Napoleon Hill

12.1 Getting Your Ideas Down

When I have to present a new topic, sometimes I feel a bit overwhelmed - there's so much to say and I don't know where to begin. What should I include, what's out of scope? How much detail? When I have that feeling of being paralyzed by the enormity of it all, I turn to "mind maps." Within a few minutes, my paralysis is cured and I'm on a roll.

Mind maps help generate and organize your ideas. If you google "mind maps," you'll find pages and pages on mind mapping techniques and applications.

To get started, you can download a free mind-mapping

software application. My current favorite is the free version of xMind (www.xmind.net) but you might want to do your own research to see what's out there.

By the way, you don't have to build a mind map using software. You can create one on paper. In fact, if you are part of a group putting together a presentation, a blank wall and post-it notes works well to quickly get the group to organize its collective ideas.

Here's an example of a mind map that I created for my presentation on advanced social media.

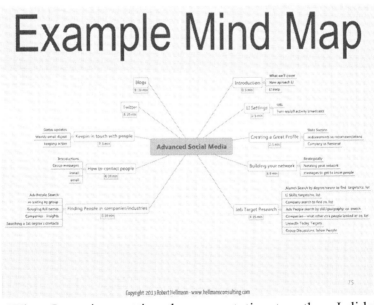

When I starting putting the presentation together, I didn't

know where to begin because there was just so much to say. Which applications should I include? What was most and least important? I thought about procrastinating. After all, it had been five minutes since I last looked at my inbox. Instead, I opened up xMind.

"Today's meeting is about Getting Beyond Group Think."

As you can see, the mind map I created is a visual way of brainstorming. You start by placing the problem you're solving at the center (in my case, how to deliver a compelling presentation on advanced social media). Then you just start throwing out ideas and placing them on the screen (or paper or wall). After a few ideas are generated, you start noticing themes, which you group together on the main branches. The supporting themes become the sub-branches. Very quickly you start moving things around and before you know it, you have a rudimentary organization of your presentation.

Once you're done with your mind map, you're ready to take organizing a step further.

12.2 How to Structure Your Presentation

In my training classes for organizations, I sometimes give attendees this exercise: "Pretend you have to present some bad financial results. How do you go about organizing the presentation?" Almost always, I get a "one-size-fits all" approach. Participants generally fail to ask themselves the key question discussed in Chapter 2: "What's the purpose of this presentation?"

In fact, what you are trying to achieve with your audience is crucial in deciding how to organize the material. There are many ways to structure a presentation, depending on what your objectives are. A few ideas follow.

Try Starting with the Hook

In Chapter 4, we discussed various options for engaging your audience right from the start. When organizing your presentation, it makes sense to grab their attention up front, using one of the hooks described in Chapter 4, section 2. I strongly encourage you to at least think about starting all your presentations off with a hook.

Why, What, How, What If

Answer these four questions, in this order, and you will

have a presentation structure that works well for many situations. This format is distilled from the "4MAT" model that was developed by Bernice McCarthy (learn more about it at her www.aboutlearning.com website).

While designed for educators and tailored for "enabling" presentations (see Chapter 2), this format also works quite well for "influencing" presentations. In fact, I applied this format in writing both this book. Let's go through each of the four parts that comprise this format.

Why: Tell the audience why they should care or pay attention, or what the problem is. This part comes at the beginning of your presentation and it's where you hook people in.

For this book I attempted to hook you into why you should care by showing you (back in Chapter 1) that what many people think is the key to a great presentation (i.e. the mechanics) is actually not the most important element. In other words, I stimulated your curiosity to find out more.

What: This is the answer to the problems or issues raised in the "Why" section. For this book, the "What" is the *RESULTS* method introduced in Chapter 2, which addresses the problem raised by the question in Chapter 1: "What is the Key to a Great Presentation?"

How: Provides your audience the detail they need to

understand and apply the solution (the "What"). For this book, the "How" is each of the chapters that describes the seven elements of the *RESULTS* method.

What If: This part of the presentation anticipates audience questions or concerns and addresses them. For this book, the "What If" includes Chapter 10 (how to apply *RESULTS* to your pitch), Chapter 11 (how to deal with presentation anxiety), Chapter 12 (how to organize your presentation), and Chapter 13 (common mechanical issues when presenting).

Opening, Body, Close, Next Steps

This approach to organizing your presentation is based on a classic sales technique: "Tell 'em what you're gonna tell them (the Opening)," "Tell 'em (the Body)," and then "Tell 'em what you told 'em (the Close)."

This structure works well for "influencing" presentations, where you are recommending a course of action. It also works well when you are presenting to an impatient senior executive of the "Tell Me Now" type (see Chapter 8). This type of executive wants you to get right to the point, which is, "What are your conclusions and what do you want me to do?" For this type of structure, you want to get to the point in the **Opening**.

Once you've satisfied their need for you to "get to the point" up front in the Opening, you can then give additional detail in the **Body** about why you feel the way you do and how your proposal would work.

In the **Close**, you summarize, in perhaps a slightly different way, the conclusion that you presented up front.

Adding a **Next Steps** section at the end ensures that everyone understands what they need to do to move your proposal forward.

Another way of thinking about this approach to presentation organization is to simply change the name to "Persuade, Inform, Persuade, Next Steps."

Good News, Bad News, Good news

Sometimes you have bad news to present, and you want to sugarcoat it to make it easier to swallow. A classic example is when a public company presents its quarterly or annual results to analysts and shareholders. If the story is mostly bad, you can bet that they will sandwich the bad news between slices of upbeat news.

Problem, Options, Recommendations

This method of organizing the presentation is almost the inverse of the Good News - Bad News - Good News approach. In this case, you want to draw attention to the **Problem** up front. In fact, you may want to dramatically draw attention to it. If financial results are bad, you may want to focus your staff's attention on the poor performance and the possible consequences in order to spur action.

Chapter 9 contains an example of how this "Problem" section might work in practice; the "$3,000,000" slide referenced on page 63 highlights how much the company was losing every year because of needless staff attrition.

For the **Options** part of the presentation, you will want to venture one or more solutions, along with details, including pros and cons. Finally, the **Recommendations** section suggests the course of action you recommend, including a summary of the benefits.

12.3 Time It

If you have a presentation of 30 minutes or more, I highly recommend that you create a timing sheet and bring it with you. Leave it on a table or podium near you, so that you can glance at it every so often. This will help you see if you're ahead or behind where you should be.

Below is the timing sheet I created for my LinkedIn presentation. You can see that I indicated where I wanted to be in the presentation at each point in time.

TIME IT OUT

Topics	Min	Total Time	Notes
INTRO, What we'll cover, Strategy	5.0	5.0	Through Get set up, then use it
NETWORK (at 5 minutes)			
NETWORK OVERVIEW	5.0	10.0	DEMO -- show network stat's HELP FEATURE
NETWORK STRATEGY	5.0	15.0	Discuss
HOW BUILD YOUR NETWORK	5.0	20.0	DEMO go to Contacts DEMO HELP FEATURE
SETTINGS (20 minutes)			
SETTINGS -- CHANGE URL	2.5		DEMO
SETTINGS- hide profile changes	2.5	25.0	DEMO
PROFILE (25 minutes)			
OVERVIEW	5.0	30.0	DECK
SECTIONS-- ALL OTHER	2.0	32.0	DEMO -- refer to book list CUT AND PASTE BULLETS

All too often, presenters try to jam too much into too little time. The result is a presentation that ends up feeling rushed or has something important left out. Neither of these outcomes is going to impress your audience. Periodically glancing at a timing sheet while you are going through your presentation will help keep you on track so that you can adjust your presentation if necessary before being faced with the possibility of having an inelegant conclusion to your talk.

Chapter 13: The Mechanics

"The most precious things in speech are the pauses."
Sir Ralph Richardson
(English Stage Actor)

"Well-timed silence hath more eloquence than speech."
Martin Farquhar Tupper
(19th Century English Writer and Poet)

As mentioned in Chapter 1, you need to get feedback on how you come across physically to be certain you aren't damaging an otherwise great presentation. There is no one-size-fits-all approach to the mechanics, as most of us bring our own particular quirks to how we present.

For example, a client once told me, "Rob, I don't feel like I'm connecting with the audience in my presentations. Can you help me?" I went to listen to him speak and the problem was immediately clear. He was so soft-spoken that the audience literally couldn't hear him. That was a mechanical issue. Once he fixed that, he was fine.

Another client was getting stuck in interview situations. She said to me, "Rob, I don't know what the problem is. I can't seem to close the deal." She sounded fine over the phone, and so I didn't understand what was wrong. I suggested that we meet.

Within 5 minutes I knew what the issue was. She wasn't making eye contact. It turned out that she had been working in the same company for 20 years and they had gotten used to her quirk, but now that she was in the interview process, it wasn't working for her anymore. I made her aware of the problem and showed her some "eye-contact" exercises. Problem solved - she started getting offers.

How do you get feedback about your presenting style? One suggestion is that you join *Toastmasters,* a great, inexpensive resource for practicing to become a better presenter and getting critiqued. If you google "Toastmasters" you will see they have chapters all over the world. I used to be a member myself.

Another idea: Ask people after you give a presentation, "How did I come across?"

Hellmann Career Consulting also offers organizational workshops and private coaching.

Below I share the most common mechanical issues that I've observed in presentations.

Deer in Headlights
One of my clients, a business development executive, was very personable, really a pleasure to talk with. As soon as

she put herself into "presentation mode," however, she became wooden and impersonal. Her "frozen" demeanor reminded me of a deer caught in oncoming headlights. It was amazing to see the transformation that took place, solely because of a shift inside of her head.

Here's how we overcame this problem. I asked her to tell me a story about something in her life that really mattered to her. She told me about an incident involving her son, how she helped him to overcome an obstacle at school, and how she was so proud of him. While she was telling me the story, she resumed her default warm, personable delivery. I was moved by her description of how she helped her son.

As soon as she finished sharing this story, I asked her to make a mental note of how she felt, and how she behaved physically during her delivery. Then I asked her to once again begin her presentation, but this time

1) Emulate the same delivery that she used when talking about her son.
2) "Pretend" that the material she was sharing was vital for the audience to hear.

The result was an immediate, dramatic improvement. I've tried the same approach with other clients who have been caught in the headlights, with similar, positive results.

I Must Protect Myself!

Many presenters channel their presentation anxiety into unnatural poses, like presenting with their arms crossed, either just below their chest or in front of their crotch. Crossing your arms in this way appears defensive to the audience, betraying a nervousness that hurts your credibility.

The solution? a) Don't do it! And b) apply the two-step "Deer in Headlights solution" that we just discussed.

What Are These Things?

There is a hilarious scene in the TV show "30 Rock" where Jack Donaghy (Alec Baldwin) is being filmed for a TV spot, and suddenly he doesn't know what to do with his arms (google "30 Rock over thinking your acting" to watch the clip on YouTube). Many of us, when we get nervous while presenting, don't know what to do with our arms. The result manifests itself in either an unnatural rigidity or overuse/flailing.

The way you deal with this problem is to a) apply the "Deer in Headlights Solution" and b) keep in mind that when you are naturally using your arms, they are usually not farther apart than the width of a globe of the world. So if you pretend that you are holding a globe, your arms won't look unnaturally far apart.

I Don't Care for You

Ever watch a presenter who never looks at the audience? Maybe s/he's too busy looking up at the slides or down at notes, or looking at something way over the audience's head. To the audience, this kind of body language conveys a lack of interest in them.

Remember to always face the audience, but shift your attention every 10 seconds or so to different parts of the audience, making sure you're not leaving anyone out.

Playing Around

I have watched many presenters engage in distracting behavior up on stage. Most of the time this behavior involves fiddling with something. I've seen presenters play with their pens, paperclips, jewelry, hair, clothes, and their hands—intertwining them, bending them back and forth, etc. Don't do it!

UpTalk

Some people speak in a way where every sentence sounds like it's ending in a question? Even when no question is asked, the sounds go "up" at the end of the sentence?

If you engage in this "UpTalk," know that you will sound less authoritative, and unsure of yourself. You can google

"UpTalk" or do a similar search on YouTube to find many examples of what it sounds like. As an alternative, practice having the sound of your voice drop down at the end of a sentence. You will sound much more authoritative.

Um...

Um, Ahh, right, ok, you-know... presenters utilize these to fill gaps, and using them regularly in your speech can quickly become a habit. Used too often in a presentation, they can become distracting and betray nervousness. Record yourself presenting and listen for too many of these filler words and sounds. If you have this problem, the solution is to create a new habit. Put a sign over your desk or by your phone with the offending phrases listed. Then practice, practice, practice being aware of them in your everyday speech until you eliminate them.

Pacing of Speech

From my experience, a lot of speakers share two problems that are really two sides of the same coin. They speak too fast and/or they don't pause in between sentences or phrases to let the audience catch up. I, myself, tend to be a fast talker, but I have learned to pause strategically and frequently, and it makes all the difference.

Let's take a look at an example: Steve Job's 2005

Commencement Speech at Stanford University is widely cited as an example of excellent oratory. It took him about a minute to read the passage I have displayed in Appendix A. Based on my own research on great speakers and their pacing, Steve is right in the middle of the pack. So, it should take you anywhere from 50 to 70 seconds to read this passage. Complete it in less than 50 seconds and you're speaking too fast. Take longer than 70 seconds, you're speaking too slowly and you risk boring the audience.

The direct link to Steve Jobs' entire inspiring commencement address is in Appendix B, along with other helpful resources. Listen to his phrasing, how he uses pauses and how much of the speech is composed of stories (more on story-telling in Chapter 5). You can learn a lot from it.

Chapter 14: Digging Deeper

The *RESULTS* method will help you with both "enabling" (e.g. instructing, teaching) and "influencing" (e.g. selling, persuading) presentations. If you use this method, your presentations will quickly and dramatically improve.

This book has given you areas on which to focus in your effort to achieve presentation greatness. In my *PEAK Presentations*™ training sessions, we cover a lot more ground:

- Participants get to practice what they're learning and get immediate feedback on all aspects of their delivery, including mechanical issues.

- Training is customized, so that participants get to work on problems and presentations that are directly relevant to their (or their organization's) needs.

- Numerous individual and group exercises reinforce the learning.

- Participants get videotaped so they can see for themselves their areas for improvement, while working with the instructor.

- Diverse delivery channels and presentation props are discussed.

- One-on-one coaching options are available as part of these sessions, or as follow-up.

Please visit www.hellmannconsulting.com for more information on how *Hellmann Career Consulting* can help you or your organization with presentation skills.

Feel free to e-mail me with any questions or comments (rob@hellmannconsulting.com), I would love to hear from you!

Your interest in this book is much appreciated. I wish you success with your presentations, and contentment and happiness in your career!

APPENDIX A: Pacing Exercise

One minute of Steve Jobs' 2005 Stanford Commencement Address (it should take you 50-70 seconds)

Today I want to tell you three stories from my life. That's it. No big deal. Just three stories.

The first story is about connecting the dots.

I dropped out of Reed College after the first 6 months, but then stayed around as a drop-in for another 18 months or so before I really quit. So why did I drop out?

It started before I was born. My biological mother was a young, unwed college graduate student, and she decided to put me up for adoption. She felt very strongly that I should be adopted by college graduates, so everything was all set for me to be adopted at birth by a lawyer and his wife.

Except that when I popped out they decided at the last minute that they really wanted a girl. So my parents, who were on a waiting list, got a call in the middle of the night asking: "We have an unexpected baby boy; do you want him?" They said: "Of course."

APPENDIX B: Resources

Hellmann Career Consulting's website (blog, workshops, research resources): www.hellmannconsulting.com

If the links below are too long to type, or they no longer work, you can find them by googling the descriptions.

- Ted Talks: www.ted.com/talks for examples of great presentations. Also, check out 11 Must-see Ted Talks: http://www.ted.com/playlists/77/11_must_see_ted_talks

- Toastmasters: www.toastmasters.com

- Nancy Duarte's Analysis of Great Speeches: http://www.ted.com/talks/nancy_duarte_the_secret_str ucture_of_great_talks

Specific examples of great talks:

- Steve Jobs' 2005 Stanford Commencement Speech: http://news.stanford.edu/news/2005/june15/jobs-061505.html

- Steve Jobs handling a rude questioner from the audience (google "Steve Jobs Insult Response): http://www.youtube.com/watch?v=FF-tKLISfPE

- The Girl Who Silenced the World: http://www.karmatube.org/videos.php?id=433

- John F. Kennedy's speech at Rice University about going to the moon: http://www.jfklibrary.org/Asset-Viewer/MkATdOcdU06X5uNHbmqm1Q.aspx

Excellent overview of "The Two Minute Pitch" as it pertains to job interviewing in the book: *Mastering the Job Interview and Winning the Money Game* by Kate Wendleton (The Five O'Clock Club – www.fiveoclockclub.com).

Amy Cuddy at Harvard discusses how your posture can affect confidence, in
- *"Amy Cuddy Takes a Stand,"* The New York Times September 19th 2014,
- Amy Cuddy's TED Talk: (http://www.ted.com/talks/amy_cuddy_your_body_language_shapes_who_you_are).

Examples of companies that provide game-based training software:

- Softworks "Bravo" at
  http://www.c3softworks.com/products/classroom/bravo-classroom/

- Learningware's "Gameshow Pro" at
  http://learningware.com/gameshowpro/index.html

NOTES PAGE

NOTES PAGE

NOTES PAGE

17533727R00065

Made in the USA
Middletown, DE
29 January 2015